Reycraft Books
55 Fifth Avenue
New York, NY 10003

Reycraftbooks.com

Reycraft Books is a trade imprint and
trademark of Newmark Learning, LLC.

Text © 2022 Judy Goldman

Educators and Librarians: Our books may be purchased in bulk for promotional,
educational,or business use. Please contact sales@reycraftbooks.com.

Library of Congress Control Number: 2022906746

Photo Credits: Photographs by Ilán Rabchinskey
Author photo: Courtesy of Judy Goldman and Ilán Rabchinskey

ISBN: 978-1-4788-7383-9

Printed in Dongguan, China. 8557/0622/19255

10 9 8 7 6 5 4 3 2 1

First Edition Paperback published by Reycraft Books 2022.

Reycraft Books and Newmark Learning, LLC, support diversity
and the First Amendment, and celebrate the right to read.

MERCADO

the Heart of the Barrio

by Judy Goldman

photographs by Ilán Rabchinskey

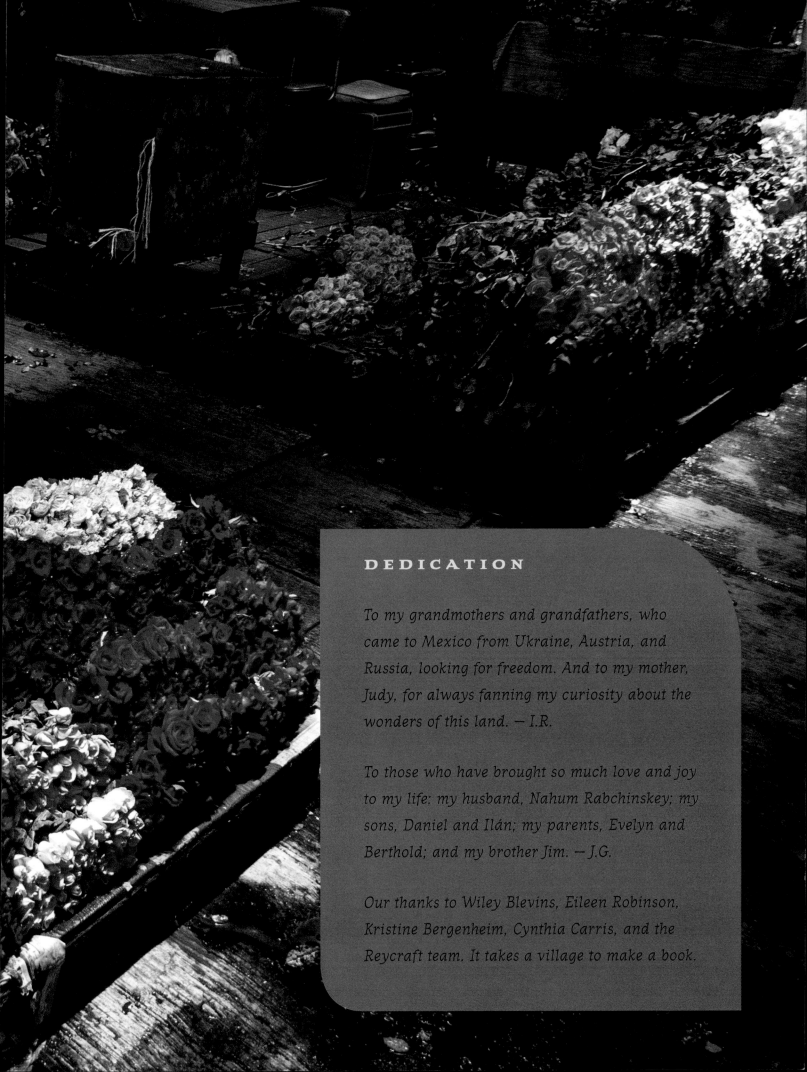

DEDICATION

To my grandmothers and grandfathers, who
came to Mexico from Ukraine, Austria, and
Russia, looking for freedom. And to my mother,
Judy, for always fanning my curiosity about the
wonders of this land. — I.R.

To those who have brought so much love and joy
to my life: my husband, Nahum Rabchinskey; my
sons, Daniel and Ilán; my parents, Evelyn and
Berthold; and my brother Jim. — J.G.

Our thanks to Wiley Blevins, Eileen Robinson,
Kristine Bergenheim, Cynthia Carris, and the
Reycraft team. It takes a village to make a book.

INSIDE THE WORLD OF MEXICAN MARKETS

Mexico's heart beats in its markets.
To enter one is to be plunged into a world of colors, aromas, and flavors. It's a kaleidoscope of vendors beckoning you to "¡Acérquese! Come closer!" so that you come near to see that what they offer is indeed very fresh. Here you can buy a bouquet of **colorful dahlias** for your home and will be delighted by the variety of **chilies** used to prepare the most exquisite salsas. It's the spot to enjoy a cone with a scoop or two of an **icy nieve** made of seasonal fruits and where you can purchase **toasted chapulines,** grasshoppers, to enjoy with the **guacamole** you will prepare for lunch.

The aroma of different spices fills the air, and your bags will slowly be weighed down with all kinds of vegetables, fruit, tortillas lovingly wrapped in an embroidered napkin, and a paper bag full of pan dulce, sweet bread fresh from the oven. Its aisles are also a great place to bump into friends and hear the news and the latest gossip.

" Because Mexico is in its markets."
—Pablo Neruda

Markets can range in size from small to huge. Over 500 years ago, the biggest one was in **Tlatelolco,** in what is now the center of Mexico City. It drew huge crowds from miles around. The merchandise bought, bartered, and sold there was vast. It included rare feathers and stones, exotic fruits and vegetables, and precious cacao beans used as coin and to make a hot or cold chocolate, prepared with water and vanilla and sometimes sweetened with honey or spiced with chili. It even included **xoloizquintlis,** the hairless dogs that were much appreciated for their company and, some say, for their meat. This market was so impressive that when the Spanish conquerors first saw the vast, vibrant, and well-organized place, they couldn't believe their eyes.

Nowadays, markets might be housed in elegant buildings hundreds of years old or can be outdoors. Some, like the **Central de Abasto,** in Mexico City, is so enormous that it has 2,000 shops spread across 810 acres. It's one of the biggest in the world. It is also a distribution center for smaller merchants, wholesalers, restaurants, and for anyone who wants to buy in bulk or just get lost for a morning in this monster market maze.

In other, more local markets, vendors show their wares—including amazing **folk art**—spread out on a blanket on the ground, usually in or near the **zócalo,** the main town square. There are also the lively traveling markets on wheels, known as a **tianguis,** that set up on a certain street on a set day and then, following a fixed route, move from place to place during the rest of the week.

So grab a few bags and let's go!

TE PARA RIÑON ACIDO URICO

TE PaRaLa ToZ. ASMA. PulMON bRON Quios

Medicinal Herbs

Almost all markets have at least one shop that offers ancestral herbs and natural remedies to cure many illnesses. Many have been employed for hundreds of years and are still used today, thanks to the healers who passed their knowledge on to the next generation. Exhibited in boxes, baskets, or mounds, each herb usually has a hand-lettered sign with its name and what it's good for.

You can find **chamomile** for stomachache, **arnica** for muscle pain, or **bougainvillea** flowers used in a purple tea to treat a bad cough. The owners of these shops know exactly where each remedy is located and how to take it. If you're suffering because your crush doesn't know you exist, they might even offer an **amulet** to make that other person notice you.

Flowers

Madonna lilies, gladiolas, nardos, chrysanthemums, sunflowers, and **dahlias,** the national flower of Mexico, are just some of the blooms you will find in the market. Some are available all year round and others are seasonal, like the fragrant **cempasúchil,** a native marigold known as the flower of the twenty petals in Nahuatl, the language spoken by the Aztecs and their modern-day descendants, the Nahuas. It blooms just in time to blanket altars, tombs, and graveyards for Día de Muertos, the Day of the Dead, which falls on November 1 and 2. This is when the souls of loved ones are welcomed back in a beautiful celebration of life awash in orange petals.

Another one is the indigenous poinsettia, the red-leaved **nochebuena,** which adorns homes, buildings, and streets during the Christmas season. Flowers are so important that there are markets--filled with buzzing bees--that specialize in them.

Fruit

In fruit stands, you will find an almost dizzying variety of shapes, sizes, flavors, and colors. Some are native to Mexico, like **papaya, zapote negro, chicozapote, mamey,** and **tuna,** the fruit of the nopal, the prickly pear cactus. Others—like apples, pears, bananas, and grapes—arrived from different countries. What you find today is a variety that has become an integral part of Mexican cuisine.

Each shop owner will arrange the fruit in wonderfully creative displays. So when you see and smell them, you'll fall in love with the perfect bunch of small **dominico** bananas, and some **ataulfo** mangoes to savor sprinkled with **chile piquín,** a very hot powdered red chili, or a couple of kilos of mandarins to make fresh zesty juice in the morning.

Spices

The aroma of **cinnamon** and **cloves** will fill the air around the shops that sell spices. **Chilies,** many native to Mexico—of course—range from mild to unbelievably hot and are used in a vast number of dishes. Many dry varieties, like guajillo, ancho, and pasilla, are stacked in huge red towers that seem to reach the roof.

Nearby are other seasonings and dry products like cumin, oregano, raisins, raw peanuts, and anis seed, some of the ingredients used to prepare one of Mexico's most famous dishes from scratch: **mole.** In Nahuatl, mole means sauce, and this black one is prepared with at least 20 ingredients. If there is no chocolate, an essential part of its preparation, it will be available in one of the nearby shops, perhaps right next door. If you prefer, you can buy all the ingredients, already ground into a powder, that you can add to chicken stock for almost instant mole!

RICO PINOLE

MOLE AUTENTICO ESPECIAL

HECHO EN CASA A LA ANTIGUA

Feria Nacional del Mole

dónde la gastronomía es un arte

Sweets

Have a sweet tooth or planning a birthday party? Head to the shop where you will find, among those produced in huge factories, the traditional ones still prepared in home-style kitchens or artisanal workshops around the country and where each region has its specialties.

It will be hard to decide what to buy—because everything looks so tasty—like round **tablets of chocolate** laced with almonds; **palanquetas,** types of brittle prepared with pumpkin seeds, peanuts, or sesame seeds; coconut-stuffed **candied limes;** huge **lollipops** with swirls of all colors; and **fruit pastes** prepared with guavas, apples, or mangoes.

One of the most famous sweets is made with sour tamarind paste mixed with sugar, ground chili, and salt, a tangy delicacy that Mexicans love and might be an acquired taste for visitors. And, of course, here you can find all the candies for stuffing a piñata.

Piñatas

No birthday is complete without one. It is believed that they were introduced to Italy by Marco Polo (who brought them from China) and, from there, they were taken to Spain. Years later this tradition traveled the seas on galleons to colonial Mexico. Usually star-shaped, through the years, the talented, imaginative artisans who make them came up with other figures like animals—even dinosaurs—and cartoon characters.

Originally, the body of a piñata was made out of a clay pot which was decorated with strips of tissue paper and then **stuffed with sweets** and hung from a rope while old and young took turns, blindfolded and dizzy, to burst it with a stick. Nowadays it is made, using **papier-mâché** methods, out of newspaper and cardboard so that nobody gets hurt when it's finally smashed and the **candy spills out,** sending everyone, amid laughter and excitement, scrambling to the ground to grab as much of it as they can.

Seafood

Almost all markets have at least one shop where a good selection of fish and seafood is offered. In big cities there are many large markets, like the **Mercado de la Viga** in Mexico City—the second biggest seafood market in the world after the one in Tokyo. But in towns all along the extensive Mexican coasts, you can find the local catch of the day in small outdoor markets.

Often, this super fresh bounty—sardines, huachinango, oysters, huge blue shrimp, clams, octopus, and crabs, among others—are snatched up quickly. One of them, the **Pacific sierra,** known simply as sierra, is perfect for preparing ceviche with lots of lime juice—which cooks the fish—as well as onions, tomatoes, cilantro, coarse sea salt, and some jalapeño or habanero chili. A most delicious meal on a hot day at the beach.

Traditional Toys and Games

When kids go to the market, the first place they head to is the shop that sells playthings, like yo-yos and tops. But the big difference with the ones that you find in most toy stores is that here they are **made by hand** and **out of wood** by artisans in small workshops. Once they are carved, they are painted in bright colors and sometimes, at purchase, the new owner's name can be added to it.

Another famous traditional toy is the **balero,** a heavy wooden barrel with a hole in the base attached by a string to a handle. It takes skill to flip the barrel and try to insert it on the stick. You might even find some of the games that your grandparents and parents played with, like jacks, pick-up-sticks, and the best shiny glass marbles that seem to hold the rays of the sun inside. In some markets, you will also find cloth dolls with delightful faces and bright ribbons in their hair. No two are alike because they are made by hand by Mazahua and Otomí women, who put part of themselves and their traditions into each.

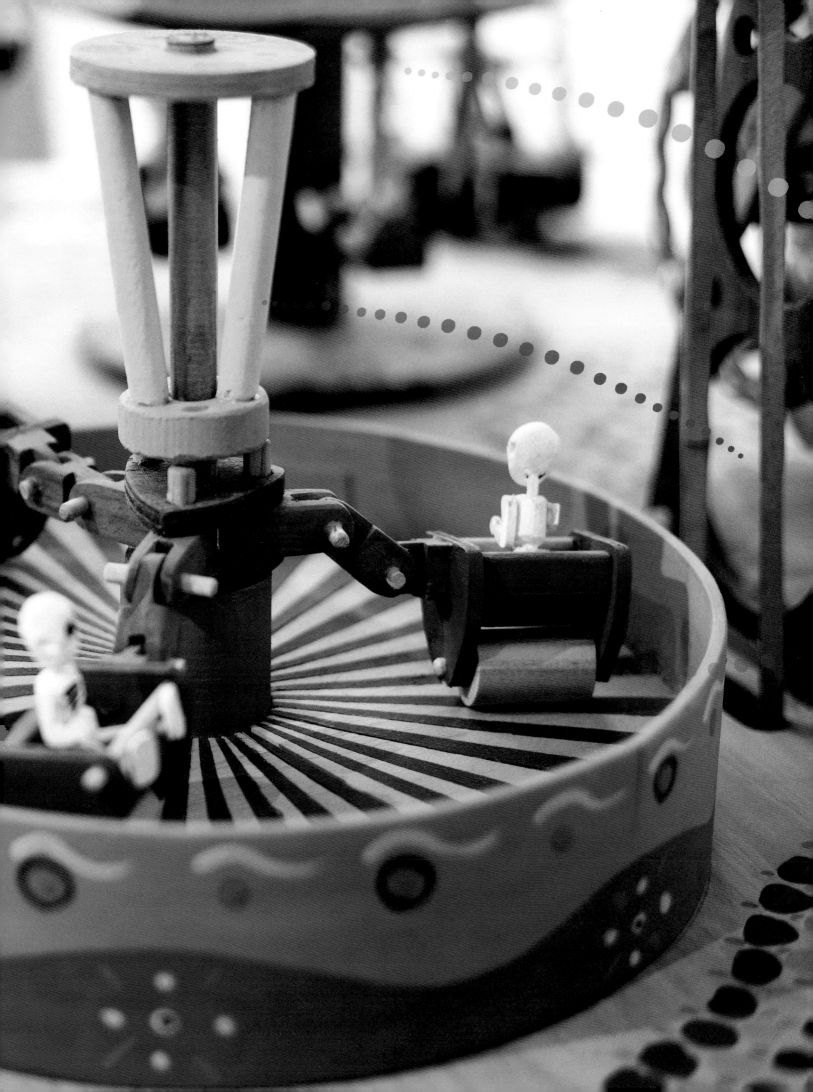

Tortillas

There are about 64 varieties of **maize,** 59 of which are native. They are used to prepare many dishes, including soups, desserts, quesadillas, and more importantly, dozens of varieties of **tacos** enjoyed all over the country. Types of tortillas are regional, but in general, their colors have to do with the type of corn used to prepare them: yellow, white, black, blue, purple, red, and green, which are made by adding ground **nopales,** the paddles of the prickly pear cactus, to the masa or dough.

In the north, where wheat is more plentiful, it is common to find flour tortillas and there is one type that is so big that it has a diameter of about 60 centimeters. While waiting in line at the **tortillería** to buy a kilo or two, people will pass the time by chatting with one another. And once the tortillas are placed in a shopping bag, most customers will take a warm one from a stack, add some hot salsa and salt, and enjoy it while heading to the next shop.

Bread

Bread is baked in a variety of ways thanks to the wheat that was brought to Mexico about five hundred years ago by the Spaniards. Some of the classic kinds of bread are **bolillos** and **teleras,** which, when split open, can be turned into **tortas,** Mexican sandwiches spread with mayonnaise and cream and stuffed with refried beans, onions, avocado, a jalapeño chili or two, cheese, and the meat of your choice.

Others are **pan dulce** with fanciful names—like conchas, polvorones, churros, and corbatas—baked in different shapes and perfect for dunking, at suppertime, into a cup of hot chocolate. When Día de Muertos is near, **pan de muerto,** a round bread that is infused with orange, covered in sugar, and with four crossed "bones" and a knob on top, appears in markets and panaderías. What better way to welcome back the souls of the dead than with their favorite bread?

Jarciería

Need a new broom or some dishcloths? Soap to scrub the kitchen floor? A mop or a feather duster to get rid of spiderwebs? Head to the jarciería, the shop that sells everything needed to keep a home clean and neat. The word comes from **jarcia,** which means products, like rope, hats, and bags, made out of natural plant fibers. In this case, the fibers are from the **henequen agave** from the Yucatan peninsula, which was known as the **green gold** because of its many uses.

Nowadays, though plastic rope is more popular, you can still find the traditional henequen kind, as well as buckets of all shapes, colors, and sizes; **jergas,** cloths made out of absorbent cotton fibers; brushes of all types; and even the bright woven plastic shopping bags that many people use when they go to the market. Some shops have so much merchandise that there is barely room for the owner to make his or her way to the back!

Vegetables

Here you will find some of the vegetables that are truly a gift from Mexico to the world like the many varieties of corn, **nopales** to prepare a salad, green beans, **chayotes, calabaza squash** and its delicious flowers, and—though they really are fruits—avocados, tomatoes, and **tomatillos** still in their husks.

You will also see vegetables that arrived from other countries such as carrots, potatoes, onions, beets, celery, and garlic, contributing to the amazing variety of dishes you can find in Mexico. And **chilies?** There are lots and lots of fresh ones, some local and others brought from different parts of the country, like **poblanos** from the state of Puebla, perfect for stuffing with ground meat or cheese; **jalapeños** from Xalapa, Veracruz, to pickle or use to prepare lots of spicy salsas to accompany all meals; and the insanely hot **habanero** which is only for the very brave.

Legumes and Grains

Every market has at least a couple of shops with huge sacks filled to the brim with legumes like beans, lentils, and chickpeas; and grains, such as barley, oatmeal, and rice. In many homes, **rice and beans** are eaten often. In fact, beans, along with squash, corn, and chilies, have been staples since way before the Spanish arrived and brought rice, which is originally from China. **Rice** is prepared in many different ways but the most common are known by their colors: red, prepared with juicy tomatoes; green, with added poblano chilies; and white.

Beans, on the other hand, are believed to be originally Mexican, and it's estimated that there are about 70 varieties of native types in the country. They are prepared in many different ways and are an essential part of Mexican cuisine. **Lentils** are also very popular, especially in soup. Try a bowl with added slices of fried plantain to make it even better.

Insects

It might seem strange to some people, but Mexicans enjoy eating all kinds of bugs and insects! Some are gathered during a certain season and others are available all year. You might buy some lovely **maguey worms** and put them on the grill, where they will blow up like delicious little balloons. Others are sold and eaten alive, like **jumiles,** a type of stinkbug. Warm a tortilla, spread guacamole on it, and add fried **grasshoppers.** Prepare a salsa with ground **chicatana ants,** which will give it a unique taste. Look for **corn worms** hanging out on the tops of ears of corn and then grill them.

Some bugs can be found in the traditional San Juan market in downtown Mexico City and others in small local markets where the people who harvest them walk the aisles with a bucket or two full of insects. Game to try them? You won't be sorry.

¡Buen provecho!